Millicent E. Selsam
and Jerome Wexler

MIMOSA
THE
SENSITIVE
PLANT

William Morrow and Company
New York 1978

Design by Cynthia Basil.

Library of Congress Cataloging in Publication Data

Selsam, Millicent Ellis (date)
    Mimosa, the sensitive plant.

Summary: Text and photographs describe the "sensitive plant,"
its rapid responses to heat and touch, and how to grow it.

1. Mimosa pudica—Juvenile literature.
2. Plants—Irritability and movements—Juvenile literature.
[1. Mimosas. 2. Plants—Irritability and movement]
I. Wexler, Jerome. II. Title.

QK495.L52S44   583'.321   78-15090
ISBN 0-688-22167-X
ISBN 0-688-32167-4 lib. bdg.

Printed in the United States of America.
First Edition
1   2   3   4   5   6   7   8   9   10

The author and photographer thank
Professor Jack Valdovinos,
Department of Biological Sciences, Lehman College,
for checking the text and photographs of this book.

By the Same Author and Photographer

The Amazing Dandelion
(ALA Notable Book, 1977)

The Apple and Other Fruits

Bulbs, Corms, and Such

The Carrot and Other Root Vegetables

The Harlequin Moth, Its Life Story
(ALA Notable Book, 1976)

Maple Tree

Peanut
(ALA Notable Book, 1969)

Popcorn

The Tomato and Other Fruit Vegetables

Vegetables from Stems and Leaves

For Deborah Peterson

If anyone asked you, "Do plants move?"
you would probably say no,
because most plants you know stay in one place.
However, many plants
have parts that twist, bend, open, or close.

The leaves of the peanut plant
are open during the day.
At night they fold up into a "sleeping" position.

Another common plant, the wood sorrel, or *Oxalis*,
closes its leaves at night too.
Each leaflet folds like a butterfly wing.
This plant is sometimes known as the Irish shamrock.

Bean and clover plants also fold their leaves at night.
If you have plants in your house or apartment,
you may be able to find other plants among them
whose leaves move at night.

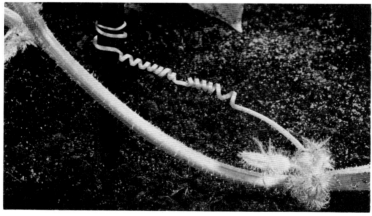

Squash, cucumbers, melons, pumpkins, and gourds
have tendrils (threadlike parts of the plant)
that are sensitive to touch.
They grab hold of any support
with which they come in contact.

The picture shows the tendril of a cucumber plant
before and after it attached itself to a support.

Flowers can move too.
At night the dandelion flowers close up.

But few plants can equal
Mimosa pudica, the sensitive plant,
in its power to move.

It can go from this

to this in a second!

Watching a plant move with such speed
is almost eerie.
Because it moves so fast,
it is called the "sensitive plant."
The mimosa name was given to it
because *mimos* in Greek means a mimic, or imitator,
and the scientists who named it
thought that this plant's movements
imitated an animal's movements.

This picture shows
what a mature *Mimosa pudica* plant looks like.
The plant is low growing
with delicate green leaves and pink flowers.
It is found all over the tropics
of Asia, Africa, and South America.

13

Each leaf has a leafstalk
and is divided into four sprays.
Each spray has many leaflets on each side.

Here is one leaf.
It is called "compound,"
because it is made up of many leaflets.

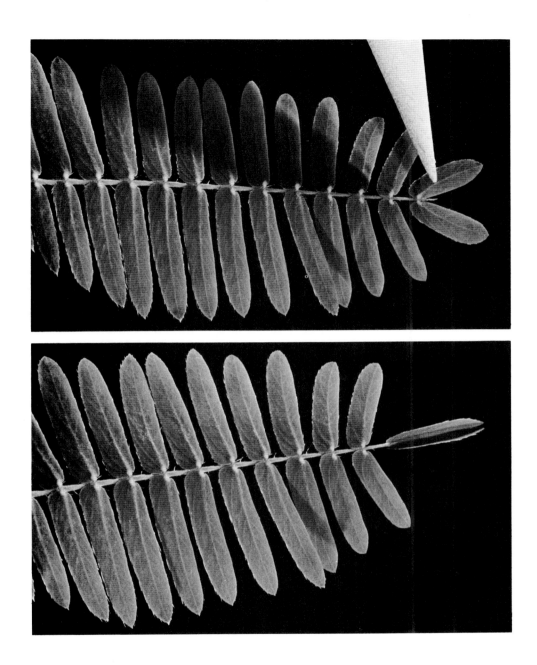

Touch the outermost pair of leaflets lightly,
and the two fold together.

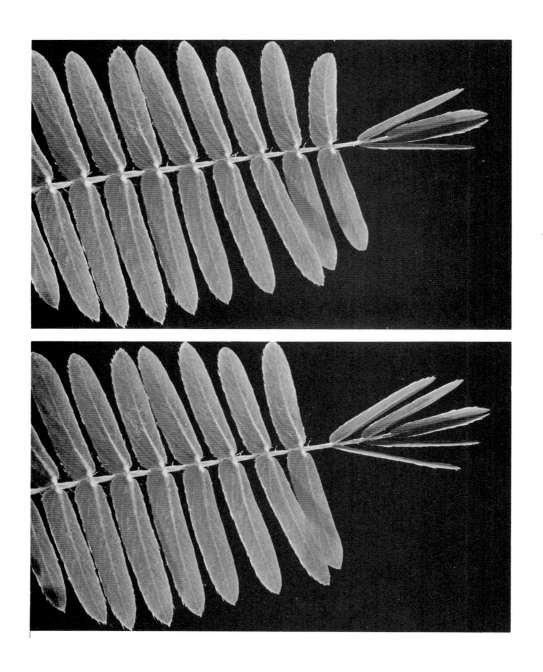

Then, pair by pair, the other leaflets close.

Some sort of signal travels from one pair to another.

A stronger touch on the leaf
makes the leafstalk bend down
at the point where it is attached to the main stem.
The same thing happens
if you hit the stem of the leaf directly.

If you shake the plant or hit the main stem hard,
the signal travels up and down
through the entire plant.
All the leaflets close, and all the leafstalks fall.
The whole plant looks closed up.

Mimosa also reacts to heat.
Here a lighted match
is being held a few inches from the leaf,
and the pair of leaflets nearest the heat
has already closed.

Then the "message" travels down the stalk,
and pair by pair the leaflets close
the way a stack of cards collapses.

But that is not all.
The message travels to the base of the leafstalk,
and the entire leaf droops.
The leaflets on the other sprays close up too.

If you hold a lighted match
about two inches from the leafstalk,
the entire leaf droops and the leaflets close.

The message then travels up and down
the woody stem,
and all the leaves droop and close their leaflets.

AFTER FIFTEEN MINUTES

The plants recover
in about fifteen minutes to a few hours.
The amount of time depends on
whether the stimulus is heat or touch,
which part of the plant is stimulated,
and how strong the stimulus is.

In the last experiment,
when heat was applied to the leafstalk,
the plant took one and a half hours to recover.

24

AFTER ONE HOUR

Here the stem was jarred and all the leaflets closed.
But the plant started to recover fifteen minutes later.

Notice that the flowers do not droop like the leaves.
This plant is pollinated by insects.
If the flower closed up when the insect landed,
the insect would not be able to reach the pollen.

Mimosa leaves also close up at night,
and the leafstalks rise.
Look at a mimosa plant
when the sky starts to grow dark.
Note the time the leaflets close.
As the day grows longer,
mimosa will stay open longer.

You can make mimosa close up during the day.
Just place it in a big cooking pot,
and cover it to keep the light out.
In one hour the leaflets are closed.
Be sure to notice how the leafstalks rise.

PULVINUS

Why is mimosa able to move so fast when touched?
If you use a magnifying glass and look closely,
you can see a special swelling
called a "pulvinus" (pull-vigh'-nuss)
at the base of each leaflet,
where the spray of leaflets joins the leafstalk,
and at the base of each leaf.

PULVINUS

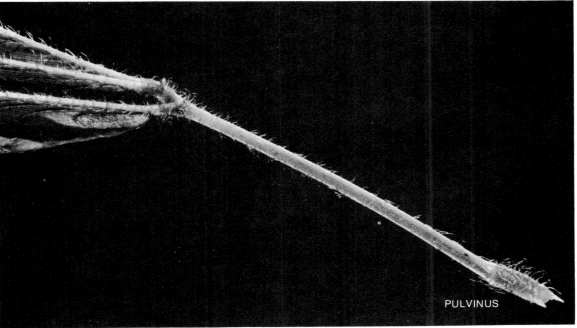

PULVINUS

The pulvinus cells are swollen with liquid
and are the sensitive organs of the plant.
When the plant is touched, or when heat is applied,
the liquid in the *lower half* of the pulvinus
suddenly leaves these cells
and goes into the spaces around the cells.

When cells lose water, they collapse.
The pictures show how the leafstalk bends down
toward the collapsed cells.

In the leaflets,
the upper sides of the pulvini shrink
so the leaflets close upward.

30

Scientists still do not know
how the message moves
through the plant so rapidly.

Some think it is electrical, like the messages
that travel through the nervous system of an animal.

Some think it is a chemical, such as a hormone.

Some think that something happens
to the membranes around the cells in the pulvinus
and lets the fluid out.

Some think there are special organs
in the cells of the pulvinus
that pump the fluids out.

Potassium salt helps
to keep the cells filled with water.
Some think that the cells collapse
because this salt moves out of them
into the spaces between the cells.

Perhaps someday
several of these explanations will be combined
to explain the mimosa's rapid movement.

You can have a lot of fun with mimosa
if you grow the plant yourself.
Get the seeds through a seedhouse catalogue.
Or you can find them
in display racks of seeds in the springtime.
The seeds should be planted in a mixture
of half sterile potting soil and half vermiculite.
Both soil and vermiculite
can be bought in the five-and-ten.
Vermiculite looks like a pearly cereal.
It helps to hold water and loosens up the soil
so that air can reach the roots.
The seeds are flat and should be covered
with only a quarter inch of soil.
Keep the soil moist.

The seeds germinate
within two weeks.
Here the seedling has just
come through the ground.
The seed coat
is popping off at the top.

COTYLEDONS

The first two fleshy leaves that show
are seed leaves, or cotyledons.
They are full of stored food
that the young plant uses as it grows.

At this point,
put the plants on a bright or sunny windowsill.
Remember to keep the soil moist.

TRUE LEAF

The first true leaf
emerges and opens.

More leaves
and flowers form.

Two flower buds
are produced
where the leafstalks
join the main stem.

One flower matures before the other.

Each flower is really a cluster of small flowers.
The buds open from bottom to top.

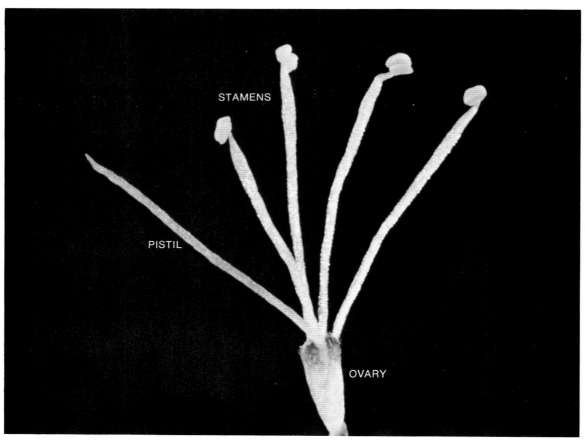

 ACTUAL SIZE

Each flower is only about one quarter of an inch long.
It has four stamens, the male parts of the flower
that bear the pollen sacs.
The part that has no pollen sac is the top of the pistil,
the female part of the flower.
At the bottom of the pistil
there is an ovary containing ovules.

The pollen from the stamens
is transferred to the pistil by insects.

Indoors you can do the pollinating yourself.
Using a small paintbrush, touch the pollen sacs
and then touch the brush to the top of the pistils.

Each pollen grain puts out its own pollen tube
that grows down the pistil to the ovules at the bottom.
The contents of each pollen tube
join with the contents of each ovule.
This process is called "fertilization."
Now the ovules can develop into seeds,
and the ovary around them can become a fruit.

After pollination, the flowers bend downward.

The fruits become pods,
like the pods of the green pea.

In this photograph,
you can see the seeds developing inside the pod.

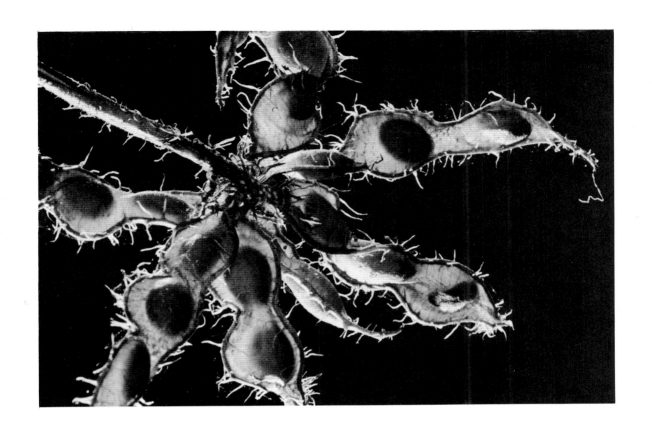

The pods spread out from each other and dry out.

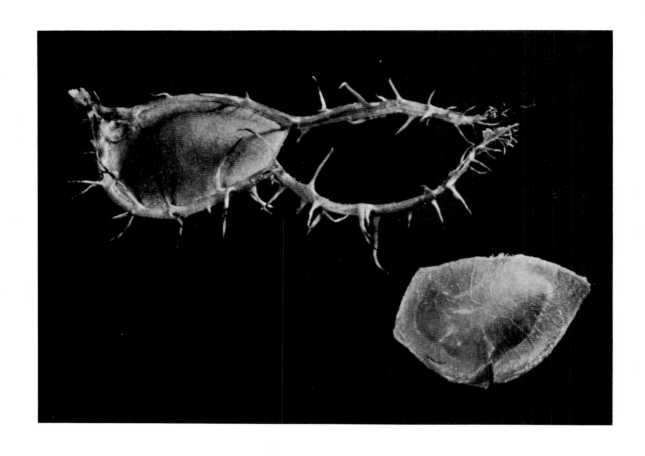

Now the seeds pop out of the pod.
This seed still has the pod cover around it.

When a seed germinates, it leaves two covers behind.
The cover on the right in this picture is the pod cover.
The one at the top of the seed is the seed cover.

Even if you have never grown a single plant before,
try growing mimosa.
You don't have to wait till the plant is big
before you enjoy it.
In about a month you will have a plant
that closes up when you touch it.
The first time you see it do so, you will be surprised,
even though you have read what to expect.
It will surprise your friends too!

Since even the scientists who work on plants
still are not sure what causes the mimosa's movements,
perhaps you can help to find the answer.

DATE DUE

JUN 1 9 1979				
V X SEP 1979				
Jul 27'79	599			
	S.W.			
F L X JUL	?			
F L X JUL				
NOV 05 '97				